TO:

FROM:

The Fight
Against Gravity

OTHER GIFTBOOKS IN THIS SERIES:
A Special Gift for Baldy   A Special Gift for Big Tum

OTHER HELEN EXLEY GIFTBOOKS:
A Spread of Over 40s' Jokes   To my very special Husband
A Triumph of Over 50s' Jokes   To my very special Wife
The Victim's Guide to Middle Age   Happy Birthday! (you poor old wreck)

Published simultaneously in 1997 by Exley Publications LLC in the USA,
and Exley Publications Ltd in Great Britain.

12 11 10 9 8 7 6 5 4 3 2 1

Cartoons copyright © Roland Fiddy 1997.

ISBN 1-85015-938-6

Cartoons by Roland Fiddy.
Printed and bound in Hungary.

Exley Publications Ltd, 16 Chalk Hill, Watford, Herts WD1 4BN, UK.
Exley Publications LLC, 232 Madison Avenue, Suite 1206, NY 10016, USA.

The Fight Against Gravity

A CARTOON STORY BY

Roland Fiddy

EXLEY

NEW YORK • WATFORD, UK

Books in the "Fanatic's Guide" series
($4.99 £2.50 paperback)

The **Fanatic's Guides** are perfect presents for everyone with a hobby that has got out of hand. Eighty pages of hilarious black and white cartoons by Roland Fiddy.

The Fanatic's Guide to Dogs
The Fanatic's Guide to Money
The Fanatic's Guide to Sports

The following titles in this series are available in paperback and also in a full colour mini hardback edition ($6.99 £3.99)

The Fanatic's Guide to Cats
The Fanatic's Guide to Computers
The Fanatic's Guide to Dads
The Fanatic's Guide to D.I.Y.
The Fanatic's Guide to Golf
The Fanatic's Guide to Husbands
The Fanatic's Guide to Love
The Fanatic's Guide to Sex

Books in the "Victim's Guide" series
($4.99 £2.50 paperback)

Award-winning cartoonist Roland Fiddy sees the funny side to life's phobias, nightmares and catastrophes.

The Victim's Guide to Air Travel
The Victim's Guide to The Baby
The Victim's Guide to The Boss
The Victim's Guide to Christmas
The Victim's Guide to The Dentist
The Victim's Guide to The Doctor
The Victim's Guide to Middle Age

Other giftbooks by Roland Fiddy
I Love You ($6.99 £3.99 hardback)
I'm Missing You ($6.00 £3.75 hardback)